"IT'S LIKE SO MANY FATHERS AND SONS—
HE HAD HIS MUSIC, AND I HAD TO HAVE MINE."
—Carlos Santana

CARL
SANT

SOUND OF THE HEART,

OS ANA

SONG OF THE WORLD

GARY GOLIO

ILLUSTRATED BY

RUDY GUTIERREZ

Christy Ottaviano Books

HENRY HOLT AND COMPANY 🐦 NEW YORK

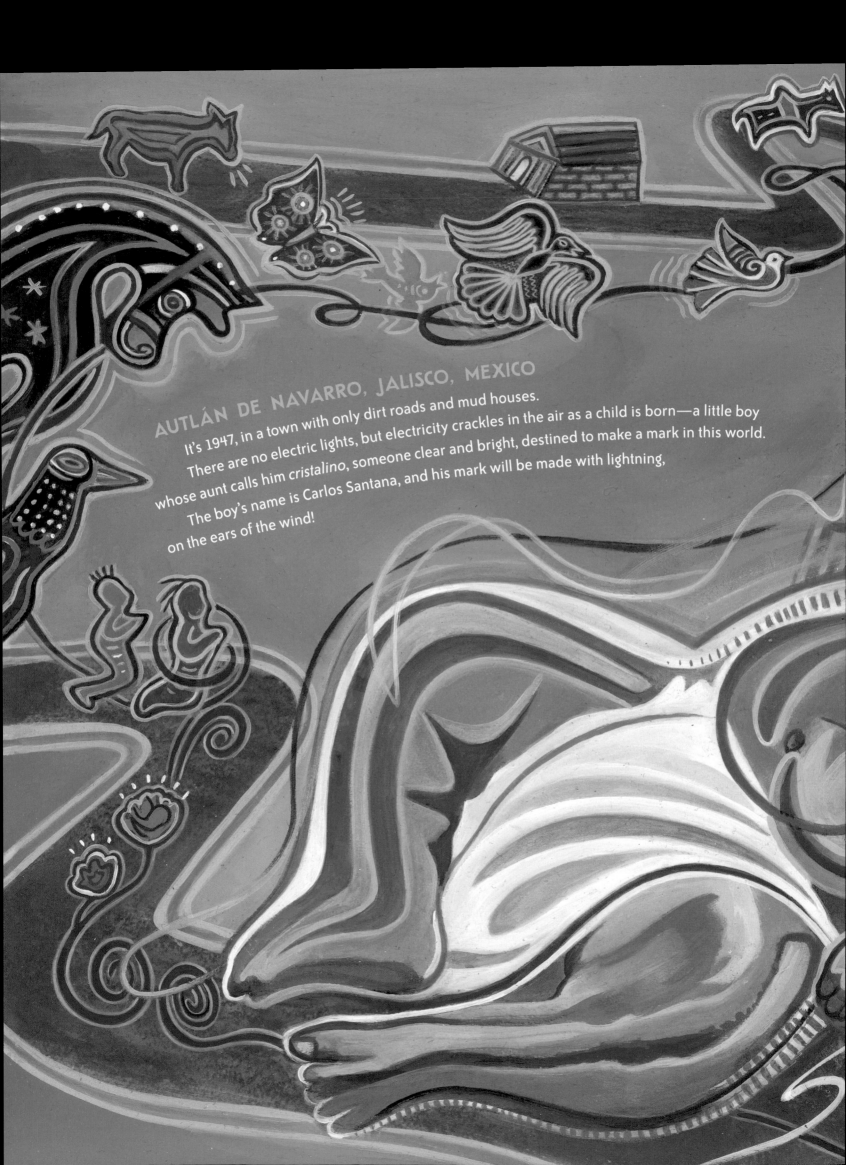

AUTLÁN DE NAVARRO, JALISCO, MEXICO

It's 1947, in a town with only dirt roads and mud houses.
There are no electric lights, but electricity crackles in the air as a child is born—a little boy whose aunt calls him *cristalino*, someone clear and bright, destined to make a mark in this world.
The boy's name is Carlos Santana, and his mark will be made with lightning, on the ears of the wind!

Carlos is wrapped in music from the time he is born. His father, José—
like the men in his family before him—can make magic with his fingers,
lifting spirits with the power of song. When Papá plays the violin, even little
Carlos can see how people's eyes light up, filled with *el espíritu de la vida*.
Everyone wants José Santana to entertain them on their special days,
and Carlos believes his father is an angel, flying on a bicycle with his golden
harp as he rides to play in the church orchestra.
Carlos loves Mamá, but Papá is his one true hero.

The fourth of six children, Carlos feels like Papá's favorite when he is taught to read music at age five, just as his *abuelo* taught Papá. Maybe he will sit beside his father in the church orchestra and begin to grow his own wings. Someday, he might even join Papá in playing *mariachi*, songs that celebrate the people and tell their stories, making them laugh, cry, and feel alive.

For now, it is enough that Carlos look, listen, and *dream*.

Yet the world is less bright when Papá is gone—sometimes for months—earning money and lighting up the lives of other people with his music. Somewhere, there is singing and dancing. But at home all is quiet, except for the songs of birds in the trees.

With Papá away, Carlos wonders how he will ever learn to play music, to follow in his father's footsteps. Unsure that he even *likes* the violin, he still wants to please Papá and keep his dream alive.

Truly, music is the sound of life, and Carlos feels its beat within his chest.

When Carlos is six, Papá leaves home again, this time for Tijuana in northern Mexico. There, in a city crowded with American turistas and music clubs, José will find plenty of work to support his family. The decision affects everyone, though Carlos and Mamá feel it the most.

For Josefina, José's journey will lead her family to a land rich with freedom and opportunity. For Carlos, Papá being gone only makes it harder to believe in music and its angels. Money comes in the mail, but money cannot take the place of a father.

Finally, after a year, Mamá makes a decision of her own. She sells all of the furniture and pays a cab driver to take her and the children more than a thousand miles to Tijuana. Four long days later, they arrive in the strange, noisy city, tired but hoping to find Papá and start a new life.

Papá is surprised to see his family—happy, but also upset that his wife has disobeyed him.

Lying on the floor of an unfinished hotel with no windows and no beds, Carlos tries hard to remember the father he knew—*angel* and *hero*—but can't forget his mother's tears.

To earn a little money, he begins selling chewing gum out on the streets.

This is his new life, like it or not.

Carlos starts elementary school in Tijuana, where the Catholic nuns are strict and unsmiling.

Still, there is a ray of light—music classes after school and violin lessons with Papá, who begins teaching him about Mozart, mariachi, and the songs of Mexico. It is tough going at first—Carlos doesn't really like the violin, and the smell of the wood, held close to his face, gives him no pleasure. Papá is also very demanding, and sometimes Carlos is brought to tears.

But he is also learning from his father what gives a musician his real strength—playing for each person one-to-one, whether the audience is a small family or an entire town. The sound goes from heart to heart, from player to listener, with a promise of respect between the two.

Without that, music is just empty notes.

At ten, Carlos is now ready to play for turistas, out on the streets of Tijuana. He dresses in a cowboy outfit and teams up with two other boys, but finds little joy in the music or the violin. Is he nothing more than a trained monkey, playing the same tired tunes day after day for a handful of coins?

Listening to the radio one morning, Carlos is struck by a sound that hits him right in the chest. It's the sting of *electric guitars* that comes from American blues music and makes his ears sizzle! Names like Muddy Waters and B.B. King seem *magical*, their songs raw and honest.

When he feels Carlos is ready, Papá brings him to the *cantina* where he and his band play mariachi. As father and son walk the dark streets together, the memory of electric guitars fills Carlos's mind. He wants his time with Papá to be like that—as fresh and exciting as American blues songs—but when the door opens, his dream goes up in smoke. The cantina is just a dingy café—with a dirt floor, a stale smell, and tables black with cigarette ash.

Holding his breath, Carlos pretends he is far, far away.

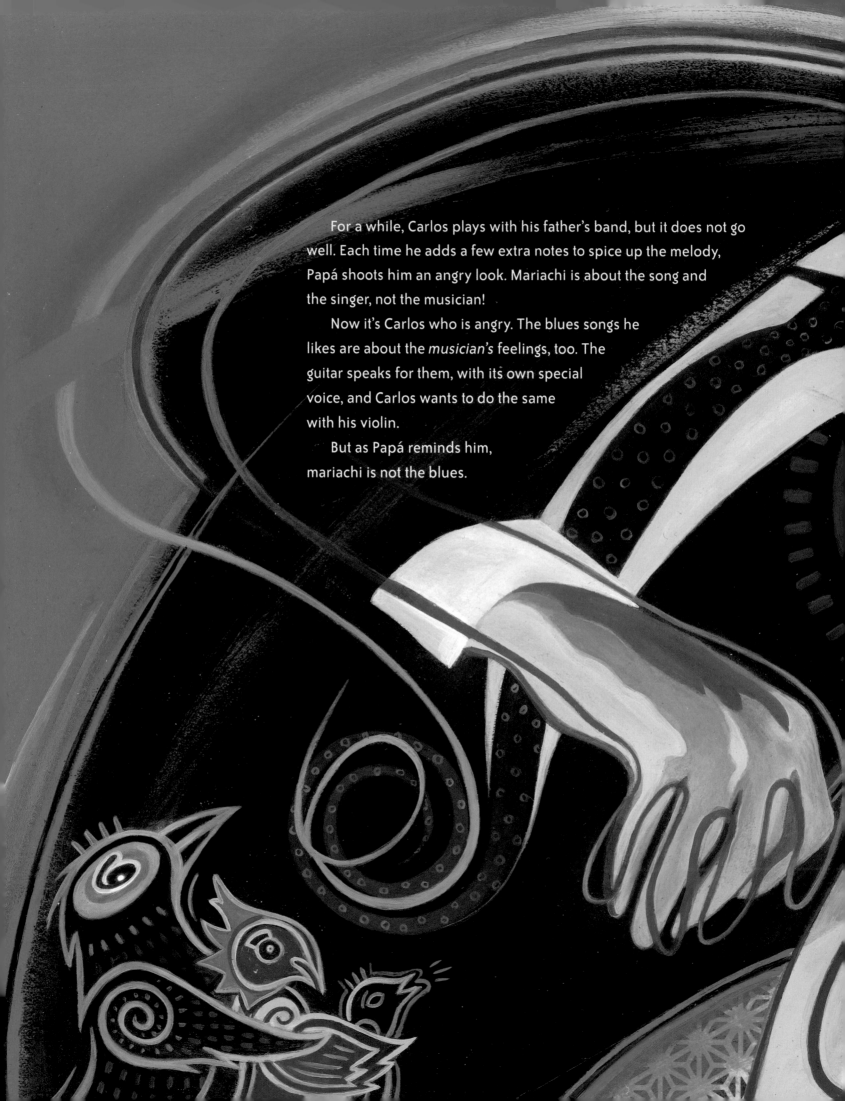

For a while, Carlos plays with his father's band, but it does not go well. Each time he adds a few extra notes to spice up the melody, Papá shoots him an angry look. Mariachi is about the song and the singer, not the musician!

Now it's Carlos who is angry. The blues songs he likes are about the *musician's* feelings, too. The guitar speaks for them, with its own special voice, and Carlos wants to do the same with his violin.

But as Papá reminds him, mariachi is not the blues.

One night at the cantina, Carlos is sickened by what he sees—men yelling at his father to play the same song over and over. They talk and laugh, and show no respect.

Though Carlos knows how much Papá needs the money, he still feels ashamed. He tells his father he's had enough, and that "when I grow up, I'm going to play what I want to play!"

Then, quietly, Papá tells his son to go home.

Carlos's nights in the cantina are over.

Back on the Avenida Revolución with his violin, Carlos is miserable. And the more he hears American blues music, the more blue he becomes. Now he can barely stand to hold the violin near his face. When Papá leaves for the US—for work in San Francisco— Carlos is secretly glad, for at least his lessons will end.

Mamá, worried about her son, takes him to an outdoor concert in the town square. It's a local band, the T.J.'s, playing the rhythm and blues music that Carlos loves. As he listens to the guitarist send electric notes flying through the air, the sounds make his heart race. Carlos feels like Muddy Waters and B.B. King are calling out to him!

After the concert, Mamá sees her son full of life once more. She writes to Papá that "Carlos's got the music bug again!" Grateful for this news, Papá buys a used electric guitar and sends it home.

When the package arrives, Carlos is stunned! There will be no turning back. Now he can start to play the song inside him, the one that has been there all along. It will be *his* song—about *his* life—played on *his* guitar.

And it will lift the spirits of all those who hear it, bringing magic to their lives.

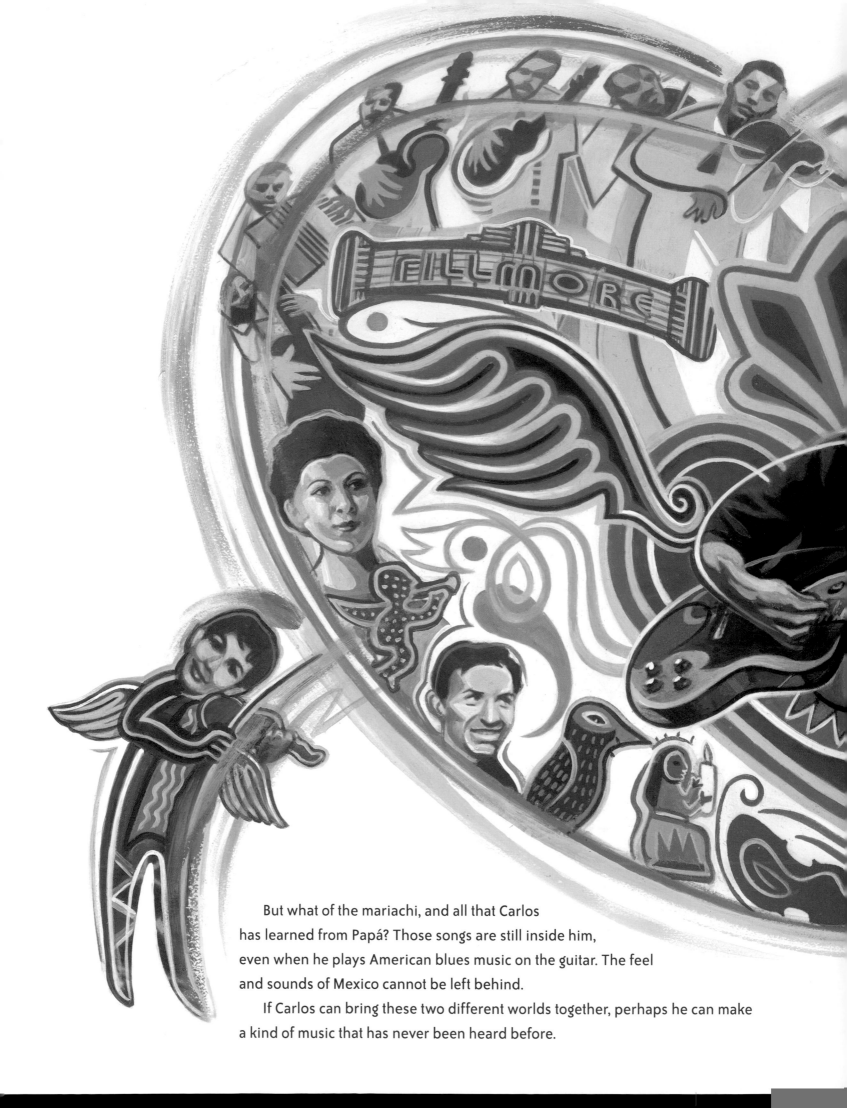

But what of the mariachi, and all that Carlos
has learned from Papá? Those songs are still inside him,
even when he plays American blues music on the guitar. The feel
and sounds of Mexico cannot be left behind.

If Carlos can bring these two different worlds together, perhaps he can make
a kind of music that has never been heard before.

Not so many years later, after moving to the United States himself, young Carlos Santana will create a new flavor of rock and roll, charged with Latin passion and the raw honesty of American blues.

Spreading out to the world, it will be music played one-to-one, player-to-listener, with the feeling and respect it deserves. Just as Papá said it should.

And perhaps most importantly, it will be music played to the beat of Carlos's own heart.

CARLOS SANTANA

As a child and teenager, Carlos Santana knew difficult times and often struggled to find his way. Taught the violin by his father at an early age, he did not feel a strong connection to European or Mexican music. Only later on—after he'd begun playing for tourists on the streets of Tijuana—did the songs on American radio open his ears to what he called the "raw and honest" sounds of black blues artists like Ray Charles, B.B. King, and Jimmy Reed. Around the age of fifteen, the gift of a used electric guitar started him off on his own unique path.

When Carlos finally moved to San Francisco in 1963, he felt a greater affinity with African and Cuban music—played by people like Babatunde Olatunji and Mongo Santamaría—than with the more popular Beatles or Bob Dylan. While he respected the blues-based songs of musicians like Eric Clapton and Mike Bloomfield, Carlos and the members of his band were searching for a different sound. Fortunately, his playing caught the attention of rock promoter Bill Graham, who encouraged him to include more Latin-based and Cuban-based (*salsa*) tunes in his playing. When Carlos and his group—simply called *Santana*—performed at the legendary Woodstock Music Festival in 1969, their innovative mix of influences won them immediate recognition and a devoted following. This new sound, a signature fusion of rock, blues, jazz, and Latin elements, set the stage for what would be Carlos's lifelong exploration of musical styles and flavors.

Today, Carlos continues to tour with his band, sharing a message of international unity with audiences around the world. Like John Coltrane and Jimi Hendrix—musicians he greatly admires—Carlos is bold and fiery onstage, and very quiet off. A humble man, he is guided by a personal sense of spirituality and a desire to make good use of his time and talents. Like his father, he strives to uplift listeners with the power of song, and created the Milagro* Foundation to provide resources and opportunities for children in need.

---

milagro means "miracle" in Spanish

A NOTE FROM THE ARTIST

I remember sitting on the floor when I was thirteen years old, digging through records as I heard the life-changing music of Santana's album *Abraxas* and saw the incredible cover art of Mati Klarwein. In that moment I sat and dreamed of doing album covers and maybe one day creating a Santana cover that would be seen throughout the world and hopefully inspire others. Many years later, that dream would come true when I was commissioned by Carlos Santana to do the Santana *Shaman* CD cover. Carlos's message of love, peace, and unity is something that I hold close to my heart along with the responsibility to use one's talent to uplift and inspire others. It is a privilege and another dream fulfilled to create the art for this book with the hope that someone will be inspired to dream like I did all those years ago. Dream on!

—R.G.

GLOSSARY/GLOSARIO

abuelo—grandfather

Avenida Revolución—Revolution Street, named after the Mexican Revolution (1919–20)

cantina—a bar in Mexico or Spain where live music is often heard

cristalino—clear, bright, shining. As Carlos's Aunt Nina Matilda said of him, "*El es cristalino*—he is the crystal one. He has a star in him, and thousands of people are going to follow him" (Santana, *The Universal Tone*, p. 18).

el espíritu de la vida—the spirit or energy of life

mariachi—a very popular mix of Mexican folk song and European dance music (with violins, guitars, and trumpets) that was played by Carlos's father and his band

salsa—a type of popular Latino dance music that, beginning around the 1960s, combined Cuban rhythms with elements of jazz, soul, and rock and roll

turistas—tourists, people from other places visiting Mexico

SOURCES & RESOURCES

BOOKS & ARTICLES

Heath, Chris. "The Epic Life of Carlos Santana." *Rolling Stone*, March 16, 2000.

Heilig, Steve. "The World of Carlos Santana." *The Beat* 19, no. 1, 2000.

Leng, Simon. *Soul Sacrifice: The Santana Story.* London: Firefly Publishing, 2000.

Molenda, Michael, ed. *Guitar Player Presents: Carlos Santana.* Milwaukee, WI: Backbeat Books, 2010.

Santana, Carlos. *The Universal Tone: Bringing My Story to Light.* New York: Little, Brown and Company, 2014.

Shapiro, Marc. *Carlos Santana: Back on Top.* New York: St. Martin's Griffin, 2002.

SELECTED DISCOGRAPHY

Santana. *Abraxas.* Columbia/Legacy, 1985. Originally released in 1970.

———. *Santana.* Columbia, 2004, compact disc. Originally released in 1969.

———. *Shaman.* Arista Records, 2002, compact disc.

———. *Supernatural.* Arista Records, 1999, compact disc.

WEBSITES

Santana: The Official Carlos Santana Web Site, santana.com

The Milagro Foundation, milagrofoundation.org

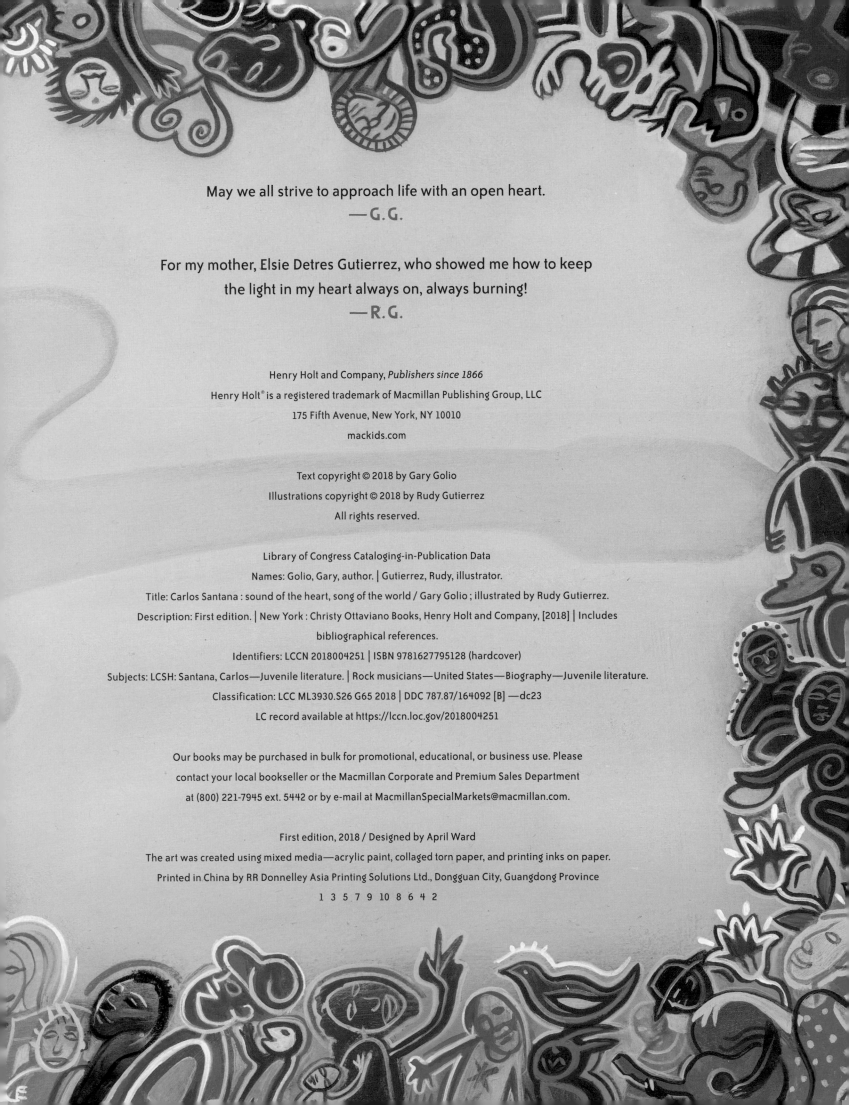

May we all strive to approach life with an open heart.
—G.G.

For my mother, Elsie Detres Gutierrez, who showed me how to keep
the light in my heart always on, always burning!
—R.G.

Henry Holt and Company, *Publishers since 1866*
Henry Holt® is a registered trademark of Macmillan Publishing Group, LLC
175 Fifth Avenue, New York, NY 10010
mackids.com

Library of Congress Cataloging-in-Publication Data
Names: Golio, Gary, author. | Gutierrez, Rudy, illustrator.
Title: Carlos Santana : sound of the heart, song of the world / Gary Golio ; illustrated by Rudy Gutierrez.
Description: First edition. | New York : Christy Ottaviano Books, Henry Holt and Company, [2018] | Includes
bibliographical references.
Identifiers: LCCN 2018004251 | ISBN 9781627795128 (hardcover)
Subjects: LCSH: Santana, Carlos—Juvenile literature. | Rock musicians—United States—Biography—Juvenile literature.
Classification: LCC ML3930.S26 G65 2018 | DDC 787.87/164092 [B] —dc23
LC record available at https://lccn.loc.gov/2018004251

Our books may be purchased in bulk for promotional, educational, or business use. Please
contact your local bookseller or the Macmillan Corporate and Premium Sales Department
at (800) 221-7945 ext. 5442 or by e-mail at MacmillanSpecialMarkets@macmillan.com.

First edition, 2018 / Designed by April Ward
The art was created using mixed media—acrylic paint, collaged torn paper, and printing inks on paper.
Printed in China by RR Donnelley Asia Printing Solutions Ltd., Dongguan City, Guangdong Province

1 3 5 7 9 10 8 6 4 2

"THE MOST VALUABLE
POSSESSION YOU CAN OWN
IS AN OPEN HEART."

—Carlos Santana